Sports Gear

• Start TO Finish

FROM

Wood

TO

Baseball Bat

● ROBIN NELSON

LERNER PUBLICATIONS COMPANY › Minneapolis

Lerner Publications Company
A division of Lerner Publishing Group, Inc.
241 First Avenue North
Minneapolis, MN 55401 USA

For reading levels and more information, look up this title at www.lernerbooks.com.

Library of Congress Cataloging-in-Publication Data

Nelson, Robin, 1971–
    From wood to baseball bat / by Robin Nelson.
        pages   cm. — (Start to finish: sports gear)
    Includes index.
    ISBN 978–1–4677–3891–0 (lib. bdg. : alk. paper)
    ISBN 978–1–4677–4742–4 (eBook)
    1. Baseball bats—Juvenile literature. I. Title.
GV879.7.N45 2015
688.7'6357—dc23
                                        2014001717

Manufactured in the United States of America
4-45440-16006-2/21/2018

TABLE OF Contents

Baseball is a blast! How was my bat made?

First, trees are cut into logs.

Wooden baseball bats are made from ash or maple trees. When a tree is big enough, workers cut it down. They cut the tree into logs. The logs are taken to a **sawmill**.

Then the logs are cut and shaped.

The mill cuts the best logs into smaller pieces called **billets**. Workers shape the billets into cylinders. Next, the billets are dried. This makes them light and keeps them straight. Then the billets are sent to a **factory**.

Next, a worker chooses a billet.

At the factory, the billets are checked to make sure they will be strong. Their **grain** has to be perfectly straight. A worker chooses a billet of the right size and weight to make a bat.

A machine carves the wood.

A worker puts the billet into a machine. This machine turns the wood very fast. A sharp blade carves the wood as it spins. The machine forms the **knob**, the thin handle, and the wider **barrel** of the bat.

Then the bat is sanded.

The bat is put in another machine. This
machine also turns the bat. As it turns,
a worker sands the bat until it is smooth.

Next, workers check the bat.

The bat has a **nub** at each end where the machines held it. Workers cut off the nubs. They sand the ends of the bat. Then they make sure the bat is the right size and weight.

Machines add logos.

Workers move the bat to more machines. One machine burns the logo onto the bat. Another machine uses **lasers** to add details about the style of the bat.

Then a worker stains the bat.

A worker dips the bat in stain. Stain makes the barrel of the bat darker. Then he or she hangs the bat to dry. Next, the bat is sprayed with clear liquid. The liquid hardens to protect the bat.

Finally, the bat is shipped.

The finished bat is shipped to a store. It is ready for the big game. Batter up!

Glossary

barrel: the part of a baseball bat that is shaped like a tube

billets: short, thick pieces of wood

carves: cuts and shapes a hard material

factory: a building where things are made

grain: the lines or fibers in a piece of wood

knob: the round handle on the end of a bat

lasers: devices that produce narrow, powerful beams of light. Lasers can be used for cutting.

logos: symbols used to identify a company

nub: a small piece or end

sawmill: a place where logs are sawed into smaller pieces

stains: uses a special liquid to change the color of something

Further Information

Kelly, David A. *Miracle Mud: Lena Blackburne and the Secret Mud That Changed Baseball.* Minneapolis: Millbrook Press, 2013. For seventy-five years, baseball teams have used Lena's magic mud to prepare baseballs before every game. Read the story of how Lena's mud went from a riverbank to the major leagues and all the way to the Hall of Fame.

Louisville Slugger Unveils New "MLB Prime" Bat
http://live.wsj.com/video/louisville-slugger-unveils-new-mlb-prime
-bat/A0EFFA71-15D3-4381-B688-792C2E399B32.html#!A0EFFA71
-15D3-4381-B688-792C2E399B32
See how bats are made in this video shot at the Louisville Slugger factory.

Nelson, Robin. *Baseball Is Fun!* Minneapolis: Lerner Publications, 2014. Learn the basics of baseball while building reading skills.

Wheeler, Lisa. *Dino-Baseball.* Minneapolis: Carolrhoda Picture Books, 2010. See what happens when a group of meat-eating dinosaurs get together with a group of plant-eating dinosaurs for a friendly game of baseball.

Index

Photo Acknowledgments

The images in this book are used with the permission of:
© Igor Vesninoff/Dreamstime.com, p. 1; © iStockphoto.com/Andrew Rich, p. 3; © Philip Scalia/Alamy, p. 5; © Al Tielemans/Sports Illustrated/Getty Images, p. 7; © Ty Wright/Bloomberg via Getty Images, pp. 9, 11; REUTERS/John Sommers II, pp. 13, 15, 19; © Ty Wright/Bloomberg via Getty Images, p. 17; AP Photo/Gene J Puskar, p. 21.

Front cover: © Walter Arce/Dreamstime.com.

Main body text set in Arta Std Book 20/26.
Typeface provided by International Typeface Corp.